Aboriginal Legends of Canada

Blackfoot

Megan Cuthbert

Weigl

Published by Weigl Educational Publishers Limited
6325 10th Street SE
Calgary, Alberta T2H 2Z9
Website: www.weigl.ca

Library and Archives Canada Cataloguing in Publication

Cuthbert, Megan, 1984-, author
        Blackfoot / Megan Cuthbert.
(Aboriginal legends of Canada)
Issued in print and electronic formats.
ISBN 978-1-77071-298-0 (bound).--ISBN 978-1-77071-299-7 (pbk.).--
ISBN 978-1-77071-300-0 (ebook)
        1. Siksika Indians--Folklore. I. Title.
E99.S54C88 2013   j398.2089'97352   C2013-907324-8
                                               C2013-907325-6

Printed in the United States of America in North Mankato, Minnesota
1 2 3 4 5 6 7 8 9 0 18 17 16 15 14

062014
WEP301113

Editor: Heather Kissock
Design: Mandy Christiansen
Illustrator: Martha Jablonski-Jones

Photo Credits
Weigl acknowledges Getty Images and Alamy as its primary image suppliers for this title.

We acknowledge the financial support of the Government of Canada through the Canada Book Fund for our publishing activities.

CONTENTS

Meet the Blackfoot

The Blackfoot are one of Canada's **Aboriginal** groups. They live on the plains of Alberta, Canada, and Montana, United States. They are made up of three groups called the Piegan, the Kainai, and the Siksika. Together, they are called the Blackfoot Confederacy.

Storytelling has always played an important role in Blackfoot life. In the past, the Blackfoot did not have a written alphabet. They shared their history by telling stories, painting on bison hides, and carving pictures into rocks. Children would listen to stories told by **elders**. These stories helped to pass on Blackfoot history, **values**, and **customs**.

Stories of Creation

The Blackfoot tell stories as a way to keep their **culture** alive. One of the most important **legends** they tell is their creation story. This explains how the Blackfoot believe the world and its creatures came to be.

Old Man has a mix of qualities. On one hand, he is a wise man and is to be respected. On the other hand, he is also known to be a powerful **trickster**.

Old Man is a main figure in many Blackfoot stories. The Blackfoot believe that Old Man is responsible for forming the world and all of the people and animals within it. He is also responsible for showing the people how to survive and how to respect the other creatures on Earth. The Blackfoot often pray to Old Man for advice and guidance.

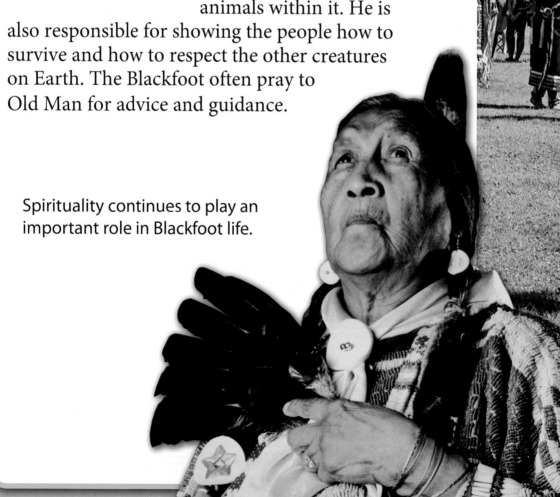

Spirituality continues to play an important role in Blackfoot life.

Today, ceremonies and celebrations, such as powwows, help Blackfoot people maintain their cultural traditions.

Creation LEGEND

In the beginning, there was nothing but water. Old Man and the animals lived on a raft that floated from place to place. Old Man wanted a real home. He asked the animals to dive to the bottom of the water and see if they could find anything that he could use to make land.

One by one, each of the animals dove into the water. The water was very deep. The animals were afraid of drowning. Each returned without reaching the bottom. Finally, the muskrat managed to bring back a handful of mud in his paws.

Old Man blew on the mud until it dried, turning it into earth. From this bit of earth, he formed the mountains, hills, and valleys. He also carved out the rivers and lakes. Old Man then moulded the first men and women out of the earth and taught them how to live and hunt. Having finished his work, Old Man climbed to the top of a mountain and disappeared.

Nature Stories

In the past, the Blackfoot relied on nature for their survival. They moved with the seasons to places that had useful plants and animals. By moving often, the Blackfoot ensured that resources were not overused in each area. This helped keep the balance in the environment.

Moving was hard work. The Blackfoot had to pack up their belongings and take down their teepees. They would then use a *travois*, or sled, to move their belongings to the next camp. At first, dogs were used to pull the sleds. Later, as *The Story of the First Horses* explains, the Blackfoot used horses to pull their travois.

The Blackfoot hunted bison and used the materials from these animals for clothing, shelter, tools, utensils, and weapons.

The Blackfoot collected berries after the first frost of the season. This is when berries are the sweetest.

The Story of the FIRST HORSES

Long ago, Piegan had a dream that he was near a lake. The lake was surrounded by animals. Piegan wanted to use them to pull his travois and carry his packs. A voice told him to go to the lake and use rope to catch the animals. When Piegan awoke, he did as the voice told him.

When he reached the lake, Piegan saw a large herd of animals, just like those in his dream. He used his rope to catch one of larger animals, but it was very strong and pulled the rope from his hands. That night, Piegan asked Old Man for advice on how to catch the animal. Old Man told Piegan to catch one of the young animals because it would not be as strong.

Piegan returned to the lake the next day. This time, he caught some of the young animals and brought them back to his camp. The people used these creatures to carry their goods and packs. This is how horses first came to be used by the Blackfoot.

Life Lessons

Blackfoot stories often contain important messages. Elders use storytelling as a way to teach Blackfoot children how they should behave and what may happen if they do not act properly. Many of their stories relate to the relationship between the Blackfoot and the animal world.

The Blackfoot believe that everything has a reason for being. They are taught to have respect and honour for all that Mother Earth, *ksah-koomi-ta-pi-aki*, provides.

The Blackfoot hold all creation in high regard. They believe that all of Earth's creatures are connected and that having balance in the natural environment is key to their survival. *The Old Man and the Beaver* shows how important balance is to the Blackfoot.

The Blackfoot believe that animals have supernatural powers. One legend tells how the Great Beaver passed on the wisdom of healing and medicine to the people.

Bison were very important to the Blackfoot, but they never took more than they needed to survive.

The OLD MAN and the BEAVER

There once was an old man who loved to eat beaver meat. He hunted beavers every day. His son warned him that the beavers could become angry with him. The old man paid no attention and continued his hunting.

One day, the old man saw a beaver slip into a hole along the riverbank. He dove into the river to find the beaver. The son followed his father into the hole. He grabbed his father by the feet and pushed him farther into the hole.

The old man thought that a beaver was attacking him. He begged to be let go. He gave it his hunting tools in exchange for freedom. Finally, the old man was released, and he returned home.

When the old man entered his teepee, his son asked him where his hunting tools were. The old man told his son that he had given them to a beaver in exchange for his life. His son nodded, saying, "I told you they would catch you." The old man never hunted beaver again.

Heroic Tales

Some Blackfoot stories feature men and women who show great bravery. They often have to overcome obstacles to help others. These heroic figures set an example for how people should behave. Their stories teach that bravery and good deeds are rewarded.

In *The Legend of Poia*, a man named Poia must go on a journey to the sky. Although Poia is an unlikely hero, he bravely faces danger. In doing so, he brings the Sun Dance ceremony to the Blackfoot people. The Sun Dance celebrates rebirth and harmony between all living things.

The Sun Dance ceremony is still practised by the Blackfoot today. An important part of the ceremony is carried out by a medicine woman, who wears a symbolic Natoas headdress.

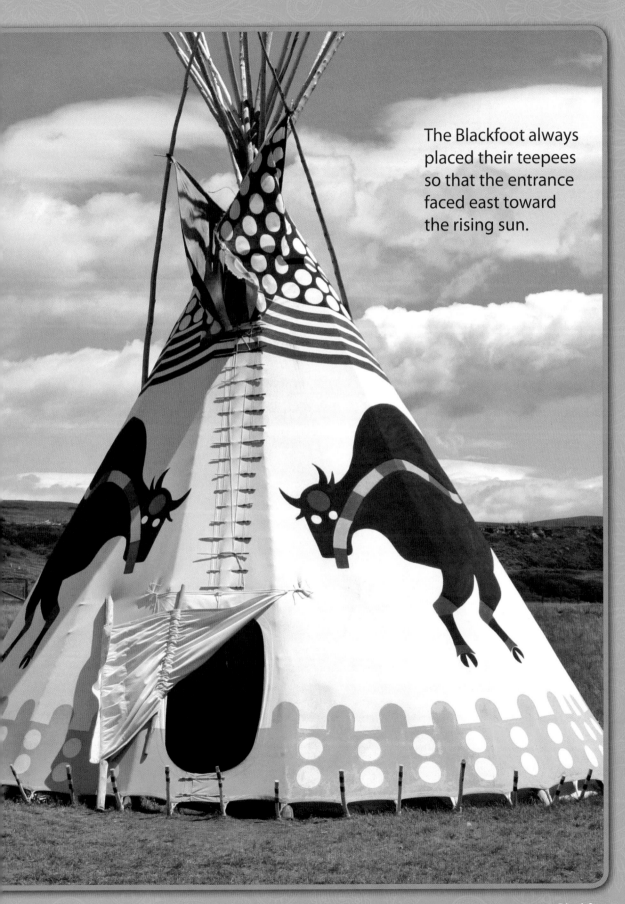

The Blackfoot always placed their teepees so that the entrance faced east toward the rising sun.

The Legend of POIA

There was once a boy who had a big scar on his face. He was called Poia, which means Scarface. People made fun of Poia for the way he looked. This made him very shy. Over time, Poia fell in love with a beautiful girl. She would not marry him because of his scar. Poia decided to get help from his grandfather, the Sun.

After a long journey, Poia arrived at the lodge of the Sun. His grandfather welcomed him and agreed to remove Poia's scar in return for a favour. He wanted Poia to ask the people to hold a festival every year in the Sun's honour. If they did so, the Sun would make the sick healthy again.

When Poia returned to Earth, he told the people about the Sun Dance. To thank Poia, the Sun arranged for him to marry the girl he loved. The couple then lived happily in the sky with the Sun.

Activity

Make a Story Robe

A story robe is an animal hide with painted images on it. The images tell the story of a Blackfoot community and show important events that took place.

You will need:

One piece of brown craft paper

Felt markers, paint, or crayons

Safety scissors

1. Draw an outline of a bison hide onto your paper. Cut out the shape.

2. Think about the events that have taken place in your life in the past year.

3. Draw pictures of these events onto your piece of paper. Try to make sure that the events are placed on the paper in the order they happened.

4. Once you have completed your story robe, make sure you share its meaning with your friends.

Further Research

Many books and websites provide information on Aboriginal legends. To learn more about this topic, borrow books from the library, or search the internet.

Books

Most libraries have computers that connect to a database for researching information. If you input a key word, you will be provided with a list of books in the library that contain information on that topic. Nonfiction books are arranged numerically, using their call number. Fiction books are organized alphabetically by the author's last name.

Websites

Learn more about Blackfoot history and customs at www. glenbow.org/blackfoot/

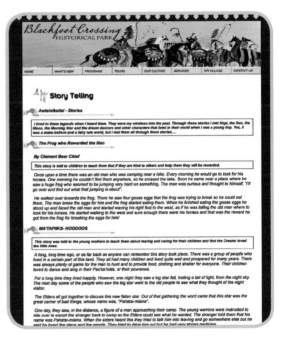

Read more Blackfoot stories at www.blackfootcrossing.ca/ storytelling.html

Key Words

Aboriginal: the First Nations, Inuit, and Métis of Canada

culture: the arts, beliefs, and habits of a community, people or country

customs: practices followed by a particular group

elders: the wise people of a community

legends: stories that have been passed from generation to generation

trickster: a creature who tries to fool others

values: what is determined to be important in life

Index